Food

A very first picture book

Consultant: Nicola Tuxworth

LORENZ BOOKS

LONDON • NEW YORK • SYDNEY • BATH

There's
definitely
nothing in
here ...

At last,
yum, yum!

This basket is *really* heavy.

Mmm ... what's this?

This apple tastes nice ...

... I wonder what this is like.

What's down here?

Oh no! Here comes Mum! Better tidy up.

Is it
lunchtime
yet?

Any chance of
some more
juice?

Please
don't wash
my face.

I drink milk for breakfast ...

... and lunch ...

... and tea!

Burp!

We're having
a tea party.

Eat it all up,
teddy!

Now for
a drink.

We're making cakes.
What goes in next?

Don't forget
the icing.

Try one,
Dad.

Spaghetti is
hard to eat.

Whoops!

We like
ice cream.

Quick,
eat it before
it melts!

First published in 1996 by Lorenz Books

Lorenz Books is an imprint of
Anness Publishing Limited
1 Boundary Row
London SE1 8HP

© 1996 Anness Publishing Limited

Distributed in Canada by Raincoast Books
Distribution Limited

1SBN 1 85967 241 8

Publisher: Joanna Lorenz
Senior Children's Books Editor:
    Sue Grabham
Editor: Sophie Warne
Photographer: Lucy Tizard
Design and Typesetting:
    Michael Leaman Design Partnership

The Publishers would like to thank the
following children for appearing in this
book: Karl Bolger, Francesca Brighton,
Milo Clare, Jessica Davis, Daisy Edwards,
Tayah Ettienne, Matthew Ferguson,
Saffron George, Faye Harrison, Zoe
Harrison, Erin Hoel, Rebekah Murrell.

Printed in Italy